Baby's Diagonal
Aran Afghans

2

9

14

22

LEISURE ARTS, INC. • Little Rock, Arkansas

■■■□ INTERMEDIATE

Finished Size:

32" x 44" (81.5 cm x 112 cm)

SHOPPING LIST

Yarn (Medium Weight)
[3.5 ounces, 205 yards
(100 grams, 187 meters) per skein]:
☐ 9 skeins

Crochet Hook
☐ Size H (5 mm)
or size needed for gauge

Additional Supplies
☐ Yarn needle

GAUGE INFORMATION

16 sc and 18 rows = 4" (10 cm)

Gauge Swatch: 4" square (10 cm)

Ch 17.

Row 1: Sc in second ch from hook and in each ch across: 16 sc.

Rows 2-18: Ch 1, turn; sc in each sc across.

Finish off.

STITCH GUIDE

🎥 FRONT POST CLUSTER
(abbreviated FP Cluster)

YO, insert hook from **front** to **back** around post of st indicated *(Fig. 3, page 31)*, YO and pull up a loop even with loops on hook, YO and draw through 2 loops on hook, YO, insert hook from **front** to **back** around **same** st, YO and pull up a loop even with loops on hook, YO and draw through 2 loops on hook, YO and draw through all 3 loops on hook. Skip st behind FP Cluster.

🎥 FRONT POST JOINING CLUSTER
(abbreviated FP Joining Cluster)

YO, insert hook from **front** to **back** around post of previous FP Cluster 2 rows **below**, YO and pull up a loop even with loops on hook, YO and draw through 2 loops on hook, YO, insert hook from **front** to **back** around **same** st, YO and pull up a loop even with loops on hook, YO and draw through 2 loops on hook, YO, insert hook from **front** to **back** around post of **next** FP Cluster 2 rows **below**, YO and pull up a loop even with loops on hook, YO and draw through 2 loops on hook, YO, insert hook from **front** to **back** around **same** st, YO and pull up a loop even with loops on hook, YO and draw through 2 loops on hook, YO and draw through all 5 loops on hook. Skip st behind st just made.

🎥 BLACKBERRY

Insert hook in next sc, YO and pull up a loop, ch 3, keeping ch-3 just made in **front** of work, YO and draw through both loops on hook.

🎥 SINGLE CROCHET DECREASE
(abbreviated sc decrease)

(Insert hook in **next** st, YO and pull up a loop) twice, YO and draw through all 3 loops on hook (**counts as one sc**).

INSTRUCTIONS
BEGINNING SECTION

Ch 2.

Row 1: 2 Sc in second ch from hook.

Row 2 (Right side)**:** Ch 1, turn; 2 sc in each sc across: 4 sc.

Note: Loop a short piece of yarn around any stitch on Row 2 to mark **right** side.

Rows 3-7: Ch 1, turn; 2 sc in first sc, sc in each sc across to last sc, 2 sc in last sc: 14 sc.

Row 8: Ch 1, turn; 2 sc in first sc, sc in next 4 sc, skip first sc 2 rows **below** and FP Cluster around next sc, sc in next 3 sc, skip next 8 sc 2 rows **below**, FP Cluster around next sc, sc in next 3 sc, 2 sc in last sc: 16 sts.

Row 9 (Increase row)**:** Ch 1, turn; 2 sc in first sc, sc in each st across to last sc, 2 sc in last sc: 18 sc.

Row 10: Ch 1, turn; 2 sc in first sc, sc in next 8 sc, work FP Joining Cluster, sc in next 7 sc, 2 sc in last sc: 20 sts.

Row 11: Repeat Row 9: 22 sc.

Row 12: Ch 1, turn; 2 sc in first sc, sc in next 8 sc, FP Cluster around left post of next st 2 rows **below**, sc in next 3 sc, working in **front** of FP Cluster just worked, FP Cluster around right post of **same** st 2 rows **below,** sc in next 7 sc, 2 sc in last sc: 24 sts.

Row 13: Repeat Row 9: 26 sc.

Row 14: Ch 1, turn; 2 sc in first sc, sc in next 7 sc, FP Cluster around next FP Cluster 2 rows **below**, sc in next 8 sc, FP Cluster around next FP Cluster 2 rows **below**, sc in next 7 sc, 2 sc in last sc: 28 sts.

Rows 15-17: Repeat Row 9, 3 times: 34 sc.

Row 18 (Low Ridge Front - first row)**:** Turn; 📹 working in Front Loops Only *(Fig. 1, page 31)*, slip st in each st across: 34 slip sts.

Row 19 (Low Ridge Front - second row)**:** Ch 1, turn; 📹 working in free loops of sc in row **below** *(Fig. 2, page 31)*, 2 sc in first sc, sc in each st across to last st, 2 sc in last st: 36 sc.

Row 20: Ch 1, turn; (sc, work Blackberry) in first sc, ★ sc in next sc, work Blackberry in next sc; repeat from ★ across to last sc, 2 sc in last sc: 38 sts.

Row 21: Repeat Row 9: 40 sc.

Row 22: Ch 1, turn; 2 sc in first sc, ★ work Blackberry in next sc, sc in next sc; repeat from ★ across to last sc, (work Blackberry, sc) in last sc: 42 sts.

Row 23: Repeat Row 9: 44 sc.

Rows 24-31: Repeat Rows 20-23 twice: 60 sc.

Rows 32 and 33: Repeat Rows 18 and 19: 62 sc.

Rows 34 and 35: Repeat Row 9 twice: 66 sc.

Row 36: Ch 1, turn; 2 sc in first sc, sc in next 5 sc, skip first 3 sc 2 rows **below** and FP Cluster around next sc, ★ sc in next 5 sc, skip next 7 sts from previous FP Cluster 2 rows **below**, FP Cluster around next sc, sc in next sc, FP Cluster around **same** st as last FP Cluster; repeat from ★ 5 times **more**, sc in next 5 sc, skip next 8 sc from previous FP Cluster 2 rows **below**, FP Cluster around next sc, sc in next 4 sc, 2 sc in last sc: 68 sts.

Row 37: Repeat Row 9: 70 sc.

Row 38: Ch 1, turn; 2 sc in first sc, sc in next 9 sc, FP Cluster around first FP Cluster 2 rows **below**, sc in next sc, FP Cluster around next FP Cluster 2 rows **below**, ★ sc in next 5 sc, FP Cluster around next FP Cluster 2 rows **below**, sc in next sc, work FP Cluster around next FP Cluster 2 rows **below**; repeat from ★ 5 times **more**, sc in next 8 sc, 2 sc in last sc: 72 sts.

Row 39: Repeat Row 9: 74 sc.

Row 40: Ch 1, turn; 2 sc in first sc, sc in next 9 sc, FP Cluster around eighth sc 2 rows **below**, sc in next 2 sc, work FP Joining Cluster, ★ † sc in next 2 sc, skip next 2 sc to left of FP Cluster 2 rows **below** and FP Cluster around next sc †, sc in next sc, FP Cluster around **same** sc as last FP Cluster, sc in next 2 sc, work FP Joining Cluster; repeat from ★ 5 times **more**, then repeat from † to † once, sc in next 8 sc, 2 sc in last sc: 76 sts.

Row 41: Repeat Row 9: 78 sc.

Row 42: Ch 1, turn; 2 sc in first sc, sc in next 13 sc, FP Cluster around first FP Cluster 2 rows **below**, sc in next sc, FP Cluster around next FP Cluster 2 rows **below**, ★ sc in next 5 sc, FP Cluster around next FP Cluster 2 rows **below**, sc in next sc, FP Cluster around next FP Cluster 2 rows **below**; repeat from ★ 5 times **more**, sc in next 2 sc, 2 sc in last sc: 80 sts.

Row 43: Repeat Row 9: 82 sc.

Row 44: Ch 1, turn; 2 sc in first sc, sc in next 16 sc, work FP Joining Cluster, ★ sc in next 7 sc, work FP Joining Cluster; repeat from ★ 5 times **more**, sc in next 15 sc, 2 sc in last sc: 84 sts.

Rows 45-47: Repeat Row 9, 3 times: 90 sc.

Rows 48 and 49: Repeat Rows 18 and 19: 92 sc.

Rows 50-61: Repeat Rows 20-31: 116 sc.

Rows 62 and 63: Repeat Rows 18 and 19: 118 sc.

Rows 64 and 65: Repeat Row 9 twice: 122 sc.

Row 66: Ch 1, turn; 2 sc in first sc, sc in next 2 sc, FP Cluster around fifth sc 2 rows **below**, sc in next 4 sc, FP Cluster around **same** sc as previous FP Cluster, ★ sc in next 4 sc, skip 9 sc from previous FP Cluster 2 rows **below**, FP Cluster around next sc, sc in next 4 sc, FP Cluster around **same** sc as previous FP Cluster; repeat from ★ 10 times **more**, sc in next 2 sc, 2 sc in last sc: 124 sts.

Row 67: Repeat Row 9: 126 sc.

Row 68: Ch 1, turn; 2 sc in first sc, sc in next 2 sc, FP Cluster around first FP Cluster 2 rows **below**, sc in next 8 sc, ★ FP Cluster around each of next 2 FP Clusters 2 rows **below**, sc in next 8 sc; repeat from ★ across to last 4 sc, FP Cluster around last FP Cluster, sc in next 2 sc, 2 sc in last sc: 128 sts.

Row 69: Repeat Row 9: 130 sc.

Row 70: Ch 1, turn; 2 sc in first sc, sc in next 6 sc, FP Cluster around first FP Cluster 2 rows **below**, sc in next 4 sc, ★ skip next FP Cluster 2 rows **below** and FP Cluster around next FP Cluster, sc in next 4 sc, working in **front** of last FP Cluster, work FP Cluster around skipped FP Cluster 2 rows **below**, sc in next 4 sc; repeat from ★ across to last 8 sc, FP Cluster around last FP Cluster 2 rows **below**, sc in next 6 sc, 2 sc in last sc: 132 sc.

Row 71: Repeat Row 9: 134 sc.

Row 72: Ch 1, turn; 2 sc in first sc, sc in next 11 sc, work FP Joining Cluster, ★ sc in next 9 sc, work FP Joining Cluster; repeat from ★ across to last 11 sc, sc in next 10 sc, 2 sc in last sc: 136 sts.

Rows 73-75: Repeat Row 9, 3 times: 142 sc.

Rows 76 and 77: Repeat Rows 18 and 19: 144 sc.

Rows 78-89: Repeat Rows 20-31: 168 sc.

Rows 90 and 91: Repeat Rows 18 and 19: 170 sc.

Rows 92-95: Repeat Row 9, 4 times: 178 sc.

CENTER SECTION

Stitch count remains constant at 178 sts through Row 132.

Row 96: Ch 1, turn; 2 sc in first sc, sc in next 5 sc, FP Cluster around third sc 2 rows **below**, sc in next 3 sc, skip next 8 sc from FP Cluster 2 rows **below** and FP Cluster around next sc, ★ sc in next 16 sc, skip next 11 sc from FP Cluster 2 rows **below** and FP Cluster around next sc, sc in next 3 sc, skip next 8 sc from FP Cluster 2 rows **below** and FP Cluster around next sc; repeat from ★ 6 times **more**, sc in next 18 sc, sc decrease.

Row 97: Ch 1, turn; sc decrease, sc in each st across to last st, 2 sc in last sc.

Row 98: Ch 1, turn; 2 sc in first st, sc in next 9 sc, work FP Joining Cluster, ★ sc in next 20 sc, work FP Joining Cluster; repeat from ★ 6 times **more**, sc in next 18 sc, sc decrease.

Row 99: Repeat Row 97.

Row 100: Ch 1, turn; 2 sc in first sc, sc in next 9 sc, skip right post of FP Joining Cluster 2 rows **below** and FP Cluster around left post, sc in next 3 sc, working in **front** of previous FP Cluster, FP Cluster around skipped right post of st 2 rows **below**, ★ sc in next 16 sc, skip right post of FP Joining Cluster 2 rows **below** and FP Cluster around left post, sc in next 3 sc, working in **front** of previous FP Cluster, FP Cluster around skipped right post of st 2 rows **below**; repeat from ★ 6 times **more**, sc in next 14 sc, sc decrease.

Row 101: Repeat Row 97.

Row 102: Ch 1, turn; 2 sc in first sc, sc in next 9 sc, FP Cluster around first FP Cluster 2 rows **below**, sc in next 8 sc, FP Cluster around next FP Cluster 2 rows **below**, ★ sc in next 11 sc, FP Cluster around next FP Cluster 2 rows **below**, sc in next 8 sc, FP Cluster around next FP Cluster 2 rows **below**; repeat from ★ 6 times **more**, sc in next 9 sc, sc decrease.

Row 103: Repeat Row 97.

Row 104: Ch 1, turn; 2 sc in first sc, sc in each st across to last 2 sc, sc decrease.

Row 105: Repeat Row 97.

Row 106: Turn; working in Front Loops Only, slip st in each st across.

Row 107: Ch 1, turn; working in free loops of sc in row **below**, sc decrease, sc in each sc across to last st, 2 sc in last sc.

Row 108: Ch 1, turn; (sc, work Blackberry) in first sc, ★ sc in next sc, work Blackberry in next sc; repeat from ★ across to last 2 sc, sc decrease.

Row 109: Repeat Row 97.

Row 110: Ch 1, turn; 2 sc in first sc, ★ work Blackberry in next sc, sc in next sc; repeat from ★ across to last 2 sc, sc decrease.

Row 111: Repeat Row 97.

Rows 112-119: Repeat Rows 108-111 twice.

Rows 120 and 121: Repeat Rows 106 and 107.

Row 122: Repeat Row 104.

Row 123: Repeat Row 97.

Rows 124 and 125: Repeat Rows 122 and 123.

Rows 126-132: Repeat Rows 96-102.

END SECTION

Rows 133-135 (Decease rows)**:** Ch 1, turn; sc decrease, sc in each st across to last 2 sts, sc decrease: 172 sc.

Row 136: Turn; working in Front Loops Only, slip st in each st across: 172 slip sts.

Row 137: Ch 1, turn; working in free loops of sc in row **below**, sc decrease, sc in each sc across to last 2 sc, sc decrease: 170 sc.

Row 138: Ch 1, turn; sc decrease, ★ work Blackberry in next sc, sc in next sc; repeat from ★ across to last 2 sc, sc decrease: 168 sts.

Row 139: Repeat Row 133: 166 sc.

Row 140: Ch 1, turn; sc decrease, ★ sc in next st, work Blackberry in next sc; repeat from ★ across to last 2 sc, sc decrease: 164 sts.

Row 141: Repeat Row 133: 162 sc.

Rows 142-149: Repeat Rows 138-141 twice: 146 sc.

Rows 150 and 151: Repeat Rows 136 and 137: 144 sc.

Rows 152 and 153: Repeat Row 133 twice: 140 sc.

Row 154: Ch 1, turn; sc decrease, sc in next 10 sc, FP Cluster around 16th sc 2 rows **below**, sc in next 4 sc, FP Cluster around **same** sc as previous FP Cluster, ★ sc in next 4 sc, skip next 9 sc from previous FP Cluster 2 rows **below** and FP Cluster around next sc, sc in next 4 sc, FP Cluster around **same** sc as previous FP Cluster; repeat from ★ 10 times **more**, sc in next 10 sc, sc decrease: 138 sts.

Row 155: Repeat Row 133: 136 sc.

Row 156: Ch 1, turn; sc decrease, sc in next 6 sc, FP Cluster around first FP Cluster 2 rows **below**, sc in next 8 sc, ★ FP Cluster around each of next 2 FP Clusters 2 rows **below**, sc in next 8 sc; repeat from ★ across to last 9 sc, FP Cluster around next FP Cluster 2 rows **below**, sc in next 6 sc, sc decrease: 134 sts.

Row 157: Repeat Row 133: 132 sc.

Row 158: Ch 1, turn; sc decrease, sc in next 6 sc, FP Cluster around first FP Cluster 2 rows **below**, sc in next 4 sc, ★ skip next FP Cluster 2 rows **below** and FP Cluster around next FP Cluster, sc in next 4 sc, working in **front** of last FP Cluster, FP Cluster around skipped FP Cluster 2 rows **below**, sc in next 4 sc; repeat from ★ across to last 9 sc, FP Cluster around last FP Cluster 2 rows **below**, sc in next 6 sc, sc decrease: 130 sts.

Row 159: Repeat Row 133: 128 sc.

Row 160: Ch 1, turn; sc decrease, sc in next 7 sc, work FP Joining Cluster, ★ sc in next 9 sc, work FP Joining Cluster; repeat from ★ across to last 8 sc, sc in next 6 sc, sc decrease: 126 sts.

Rows 161-163: Repeat Row 133, 3 times: 120 sc.

Rows 164 and 165: Repeat Rows 136 and 137: 118 sc.

Rows 166-177: Repeat Rows 138-149: 94 sc.

Rows 178 and 179: Repeat Rows 136 and 137: 92 sc.

Rows 180 and 181: Repeat Row 133 twice: 88 sc.

Row 182: Ch 1, turn; sc decrease, sc in next 10 sc, FP Cluster around 11th sc 2 rows **below**, ★ sc in next 5 sc, skip next 7 sts from previous FP Cluster 2 rows **below** and FP Cluster around next sc, sc in next sc, FP Cluster around **same** st as last FP Cluster; repeat from ★ 6 times **more**, sc in next 5 sc, skip next 9 sc from previous FP Cluster 2 rows **below**, FP Cluster around next sc, sc in next 11 sc, sc decrease: 86 sts.

Row 183: Repeat Row 133: 84 sc.

Row 184: Ch 1, turn; sc decrease, sc in next 10 sc, FP Cluster around first FP Cluster 2 rows **below**, sc in next sc, FP Cluster around next FP Cluster 2 rows **below**, ★ sc in next 5 sc, FP Cluster around next FP Cluster 2 rows **below**, sc in next sc, work FP Cluster around next FP Cluster 2 rows **below**; repeat from ★ 6 times **more**, sc in next 11 sc, sc decrease: 82 sts.

Row 185: Repeat Row 133: 80 sc.

Row 186: Ch 1, turn; sc decrease, sc in next 7 sc, FP Cluster around eighth sc 2 rows **below**, sc in next 2 sc, work FP Joining Cluster, ★ † sc in next 2 sc, skip next 2 sc to left of FP Cluster 2 rows **below** and FP Cluster around next sc †, sc in next sc, FP Cluster around **same** sc as last FP Cluster, sc in next 2 sc, work FP Joining Cluster; repeat from ★ 6 times **more**, then repeat from † to † once, sc in next 6 sc, sc decrease: 78 sts.

Row 187: Repeat Row 133: 76 sc.

Row 188: Ch 1, turn; sc decrease, sc in next 7 sc, FP Cluster around first FP Cluster 2 rows **below**, sc in next sc, FP Cluster around next FP Cluster 2 rows **below**, ★ sc in next 5 sc, FP Cluster around next FP Cluster 2 rows **below**, sc in next sc, FP Cluster around next FP Cluster 2 rows **below**; repeat from ★ 6 times **more**, sc in next 6 sc, sc decrease: 74 sc.

Row 189: Repeat Row 133: 72 sc.

Row 190: Ch 1, turn; sc decrease, ★ sc in next 7 sc, work FP Joining Cluster; repeat from ★ 7 times **more**, sc in next 4 sc, sc decrease: 70 sts.

Rows 191-193: Repeat Row 133, 3 times: 64 sc.

Rows 194 and 195: Repeat Rows 136 and 137: 62 sc.

Rows 196-207: Repeat Rows 138-149: 38 sc.

Rows 208 and 209: Repeat Rows 136 and 137: 36 sc.

Rows 210-213: Repeat Row 133, 4 times: 28 sc.

Row 214: Ch 1, turn; sc decrease, sc in next 10 sc, FP Cluster around 11th sc 2 rows **below**, sc in next 3 sts, skip next 8 sc 2 rows **below** and FP Cluster around next sc, sc in next 9 sc, sc decrease: 26 sts.

Row 215: Repeat Row 133: 24 sc.

Row 216: Ch 1, turn; sc decrease. sc in next 10 sc, work FP Joining Cluster, sc in next 9 sc, sc decrease: 22 sts.

Row 217: Repeat Row 133: 20 sc.

Row 218: Ch 1, turn; sc decrease, sc in next 6 sc, FP Cluster around left post of FP Joining Cluster 2 rows **below**, sc in next 3 sc, working in **front** of FP Cluster just worked, FP Cluster around right post of **same** st 2 rows **below,** sc in next 5 sc, sc decrease: 18 sc.

Row 219: Repeat Row 133: 16 sc.

Row 220: Ch 1, turn; sc decrease, sc in next sc, FP Cluster around next FP Cluster 2 rows **below**, sc in next 8 sc, FP Cluster around next FP Cluster 2 rows **below**, sc in next sc, sc decrease: 14 sts.

Rows 221-225: Repeat Row 133, 5 times: 4 sc.

Row 226: Ch 1, turn; sc decrease twice: 2 sc.

Row 227: Ch 1, turn; sc decrease; do **not** finish off.

BORDER

Rnd 1: Ch 1, turn; 🎥 sc evenly around, working 3 sc in each corner; join with slip st to first sc.

Rnd 2: Ch 1, do **not** turn; sc in each sc around, working 3 sc in center sc of each corner; join with slip st to first sc.

Rnd 3: Ch 1, 🎥 work reverse sc in each sc around *(Figs. 5a-d, page 31)*; join with slip st to first st, finish off.

MOSS STITCH & CABLES

Shown on page 11.

 **INTERMEDIATE**

Finished Size:
32" x 43" (81.5 cm x 109 cm)

SHOPPING LIST

Yarn (Medium Weight)
[1.75 ounces, 110 yards
(50 grams, 100 meters) per skein]:
☐ 20 skeins

Crochet Hook
☐ Size H (5 mm)
 or size needed for gauge

Additional Supplies
☐ Yarn needle

GAUGE INFORMATION

In pattern,
 16 sc and 18 rows = 4" (10 cm)
Gauge Swatch: 4" square (10 cm)
Ch 17.
Row 1: Sc in second ch from hook and
in each ch across: 16 sc.
Rows 2-18: Ch 1, turn; sc in each sc
across.
Finish off.

STITCH GUIDE

POPCORN (uses one st or sp)
Work 4 sc in st or sp indicated, drop
loop from hook, insert hook in first sc
of 4-sc group, hook dropped loop and
draw through, pulling tightly to close.

SINGLE CROCHET DECREASE
 (abbreviated sc decrease)
(Insert hook in **next** st or sp, YO and
pull up a loop) twice, YO and draw
through all 3 loops on hook (**counts as
one sc**).

**HALF DOUBLE CROCHET
DECREASE**
 (abbreviated hdc decrease)
 (uses next 2 sts)
(YO, insert hook in **next** st, YO and pull
up a loop) twice, YO and draw through
all 5 loops on hook (**counts as one hdc**).

INSTRUCTIONS
BEGINNING SECTION

Ch 2.

Row 1 (Right side)**:** 2 Sc in second ch
from hook.

Note: Loop a short piece of yarn
around any stitch on Row 1 to mark
right side.

Row 2: Ch 1, turn; 2 sc in each sc
across: 4 sc.

Row 3: Ch 1, turn; (sc, hdc) in first sc,
slip st in next sc, hdc in next sc,
(slip st, hdc) in last sc: 6 sts.

Row 4: Ch 1, turn; (sc, slip st) in first
st, ★ hdc in next st, slip st in next st;
repeat from ★ across to last sc, (hdc,
sc) in last sc: 8 sts.

Row 5: Ch 1, turn; (sc, hdc) in first sc,
★ slip st in next hdc, hdc in next st;
repeat from ★ across to last sc, (slip st,
hdc) in last sc: 10 sts.

Rows 6-13: Repeat Rows 4 and 5, 4
times: 26 sts.

Row 14 (Increase row)**:** Ch 1, turn;
2 sc in first st, sc in each st across to
last st, 2 sc in last st: 28 sc.

Row 15 (Low Ridge Front - first row)**:**
Turn; working in Front Loops Only
(Fig. 1, page 31), slip st in each st
across: 28 slip sts.

Row 16 (Low Ridge Front - second row,
increase row)**:** Ch 1, turn; working
in free loops of sc in row **below**
(Fig. 2, page 31), 2 sc in first sc, sc in
each st across to last st, 2 sc in last st:
30 sc.

Row 17: Ch 1, turn; 2 sc in first st, sc in next sc, ch 3, skip next 2 sc, sc in next sc, **turn**; sc in each ch of ch-3 just made, slip st in next sc (at beginning of ch-3), **turn**; working **behind** ch-3, sc in 2 skipped sc, ★ ch 3, skip sc at end of Cable and next 2 sc, sc in next sc, **turn**; sc in each ch of ch-3 just made, slip st in next sc, **turn**; working **behind** ch-3, sc in 2 skipped sc; repeat from ★ across to last st, ch 1, 2 sc last sc: 9 Cables.

Row 18: Ch 1, turn; 2 sc in first sc, sc in next sc, skip next ch-1 sp, ★ working in **front** of Cables, 2 sc in next sc, sc in next sc, skip next sc (beginning of Cable); repeat from ★ across to last 2 sc, 2 sc in last 2 sc: 34 sc.

Rows 19 and 20: Repeat Rows 15 and 16: 36 sc.

Rows 21 and 22: Repeat Row 14 twice: 40 sc.

Rows 23-28: Repeat Rows 15-20: 13 Cables, 48 sc.

Rows 29 and 30: Repeat Row 14 twice: 52 sc.

Row 31: Ch 1, turn; 2 sc in first sc, ch 1, skip next sc, work Popcorn in next sc, ★ ch 1, skip next sc, sc in next sc, ch 1, skip next sc, work Popcorn in next sc; repeat from ★ across to last sc, ch 1, sc in last sc: 13 Popcorns and 15 sc.

Row 32: Ch 1, turn; 2 sc in first sc, sc in next ch-1-sp, ★ ch 1, skip next st, sc in next ch-1 sp; repeat from ★ across to last 2 sc, ch 1, skip next sc, 2 sc in last sc: 30 sc and 26 ch-1 sps.

Row 33: Ch 1, turn; 2 sc in first sc, ch 1, ★ skip next sc, work Popcorn in next ch-1-sp, ch 1, skip next sc, sc in next ch-1-sp, ch 1; repeat from ★ to last 3 sc, skip next sc, work Popcorn in next sc, ch 1, sc in last sc: 14 Popcorns and 16 sc.

Rows 34-43: Repeat Rows 32 and 33, 5 times: 19 Popcorns and 21 sc.

Row 44: Ch 1, turn; 2 sc in first sc, 2 sc in each ch-1-sp across to last 2 sc, skip next sc, 2 sc in last sc: 80 sc.

Rows 45 and 46: Repeat Row 14 twice: 84 sc.

Rows 47 and 48: Repeat Rows 15 and 16: 86 sc.

Row 49: Ch 1, turn; 2 sc in first sc, ch 3, skip next 2 sc, sc in next sc, **turn**; sc in each ch of ch-3 just made, slip st in next sc (at beginning of ch-3), **turn**; working **behind** ch-3, sc in 2 skipped sc ★ ch 3, skip sc at end of Cable and next 2 sc, sc in next sc, **turn**; sc in each ch of ch-3 just made, slip st in next sc, **turn**; working **behind** ch-3, sc in 2 skipped sc; repeat from ★ across to last st, ch 1, 2 sc in last sc: 28 Cables.

Row 50: Ch 1, turn; 2 sc in first sc, sc in next sc, skip next ch-1 sp, ★ working in **front** of Cables, 2 sc in next sc, sc in next sc, skip next sc (beginning of Cable); repeat from ★ across to last Cable, 2 sc in each of 2 sc behind last Cable, skip next sc, 2 sc in last sc: 90 sc

Rows 51 and 52: Repeat Rows 15 and 16: 92 sc.

Rows 53 and 54: Repeat Row 14 twice 96 sc.

Rows 55-60: Repeat Rows 47-52: 32 Cables on Row 57; 104 sc.

Rows 61-73: Repeat Rows 3 and 4, 6 times; then repeat Row 3 once **more** 130 sc.

Row 74: Repeat Row 14: 132 sc.

Rows 75-80: Repeat Rows 47-52: 44 Cables on Row 77; 140 sc.

Rows 81 and 82: Repeat Row 14 twice: 144 sc.

Rows 83-88: Repeat Rows 47-52: 48 Cables on Row 85; 152 sc.

Rows 89-106: Repeat Rows 29-46: 188 sc.

CENTER SECTION

Stitch count remains constant at 188 sts through Row 152.

Row 107 (Low Ridge Front - first row): Turn; slip st in front loop of each st across.

Row 108 (Low Ridge Front - second row): Ch 1, turn; working in free loops of sc in row **below**, sc decrease, sc in each unworked loop across to last st, 2 sc in last st.

Row 109: Ch 1, turn; 2 sc in first sc, sc in next sc, ch 3, skip next 2 sc, sc in next sc, **turn**; sc in each ch of ch-3 just made, slip st in next sc (at beginning of ch-3), **turn**; working **behind** ch-3, sc in 2 skipped sc, ★ ch 3, skip sc at end of Cable and next 2 sc, sc in next sc, **turn**; sc in each ch of ch-3 just made, slip st in next sc, **turn**; working **behind** ch-3, sc in 2 skipped sc; repeat from ★ across to last 3 sc, ch 1, sc in next sc, sc decrease: 61 Cables.

Row 110: Ch 1, turn; sc decrease, skip next ch-1 sp, ★ working in **front** of Cables, 2 sc in next sc, sc in next sc, skip next sc (beginning of Cable); repeat from ★ across to last 2 sc, 2 sc in last 2 sc.

Rows 111 and 112: Repeat Rows 107 and 108.

Row 113: Ch 1, turn; 2 sc in first sc, sc in each sc across to last 2 sts, sc decrease.

Row 114: Ch 1, turn; sc decrease, sc in each sc across to last sc, 2 sc in last sc.

Rows 115-120: Repeat Rows 107-112.

Row 121: Ch 1, turn; (sc, hdc) in first st, ★ slip st in next st, hdc in next st; repeat from ★ across to last 2 sts, hdc decrease.

Row 122: Ch 1, turn; sc decrease, ★ hdc in next st, slip st in next st; repeat from ★ across to last sc, (hdc, sc) in last sc.

Rows 123-137: Repeat Rows 121 and 122, 7 times; then repeat Row 121 once **more**.

Row 138: Repeat Row 114.

Rows 139-152: Repeat Rows 107-120.

END SECTION

Rows 153 and154 (Decrease rows): Ch 1, turn; sc decrease, sc in each st across to last 2 sts, sc decrease: 184 sc.

Row 155: Ch 1, turn; sc decrease, ★ ch 1, skip next sc, work Popcorn in next sc, ch 1, skip next sc, sc in next sc; repeat from ★ across to last 2 sc, sc decrease: 45 Popcorns and 47 sc.

Row 156: Ch 1, turn; sc decrease, ★ sc in next ch-1 sp, ch 1; repeat from ★ across to last ch-1 sp, sc decrease: 91 sc and 89 ch-1 sps.

Row 157: Ch 1, turn; sc decrease, ★ ch 1, work Popcorn in next ch-1 sp, ch 1, sc in next ch-1 sp; repeat from ★ across to last 2 sts, sc decrease: 44 Popcorns and 46 sc.

Rows 158-167: Repeat Rows 156 and 157, 5 times: 80 sts and 78 ch-1 sps.

Row 168: Ch 1, turn; sc decrease, 2 sc in next ch-1 sp and in each ch-1 sp across to last ch-1-sp, sc decrease: 156 sc.

Rows 169 and 170: Repeat Row 153 twice: 152 sc.

Row 171: Turn; working in Front Loops Only, slip st in each sc across: 152 slip sts.

Row 172: Ch 1, turn; working in free loops of of sc in row **below**, sc decrease, sc in each st across to last 2 sts, sc decrease: 150 sc.

Row 173: Ch 1, turn; sc decrease, sc in next sc, ch 3, skip next 2 sc, sc in next sc, **turn**; sc in each ch of ch-3 just made, slip st in next sc (at beginning of ch-3), **turn**; working **behind** ch-3, sc in 2 skipped sc, ★ ch 3, skip sc at end of Cable and next 2 sc, sc in next sc, **turn**; sc in each ch of ch-3 just made, slip st in next sc, **turn**; working **behind** ch-3, sc in 2 skipped sc; repeat from ★ across to last 3 sc, ch 1, sc in next sc, sc decrease: 48 Cables.

Row 174: Ch 1, turn; sc decrease, skip next ch-1 sp, ★ working in **front** of Cables, 2 sc in next sc, sc in next sc, skip next sc (beginning of Cable); repeat from ★ across to last 2 sc, sc decrease: 146 sc.

Rows 175 and 176: Repeat Rows 171 and 172: 144 sc.

Rows 177 and 178: Repeat Row 153 twice: 140 sc.

Rows 179-184: Repeat Rows 171-176: 44 Cables on Row 181; 132 sc on Row 184.

Row 185: Ch 1, turn; hdc decrease, ★ slip st in next st, hdc in next st; repeat from ★ across to last 2 sts, sc decrease: 130 sts.

Row 186: Ch 1, turn; sc decrease, ★ hdc in next st, slip st in next st; repeat from ★ across to last 2 sts, hdc decrease: 128 sts.

Rows 187-197: Repeat Rows 185 and 186, 5 times; then repeat Row 185 once **more**: 106 sts.

Row 198: Repeat Row 153: 104 sc.

Rows 199-212: Repeat Rows 171-184: 32 Cables on Row 201; 28 Cables on Row 209; 84 sc on Row 212.

Rows 213 and 214: Repeat Row 153 twice: 80 sc.

Rows 215-230: Repeat Rows 155-170: 48 sc.

Rows 231 and 232: Repeat Rows 171 and 172: 46 sc.

Row 233: Ch 1, turn; sc decrease, ch 3, skip next 2 sc, sc in next sc, **turn**; sc in each ch of ch-3 just made, slip st in next sc (at beginning of ch-3), **turn**; working **behind** ch-3, sc in 2 skipped sc, ★ ch 3, skip sc at end of Cable and next 2 sc, sc in next sc, **turn**; sc in each ch of ch-3 just made, slip st in next sc, **turn**; working **behind** ch-3, sc in 2 skipped sc; repeat from ★ across to last 2 sc, ch 1, sc decrease: 14 Cables.

Row 234: Ch 1, turn; sc in first sc, working in **front** of Cables, sc in each sc behind first Cable, skip next sc (beginning of Cable), ★ 2 sc in next sc, sc in next sc, skip next sc; repeat from ★ across to last Cable, sc in each sc behind the last Cable, skip next sc, sc in last sc: 42 sc.

Rows 235 and 236: Repeat Rows 171 and 172: 40 sc.

Rows 237 and 238: Repeat Row 153 twice: 36 sc.

Rows 239-244: Repeat Rows 231-236: 10 Cables on Row 241; and 28 sts on Row 244.

Rows 245-256: Repeat Rows 185 and 186, 6 times: 4 sc.

Row 257: Ch 1, turn; sc decrease twice: 2 sc.

Row 258: Ch 1, turn; sc decrease; do **not** finish off.

BORDER

Rnd 1: Ch 1, turn: 🎥 sc evenly around, working 3 sc in each corner; join with slip st to first sc.

Rnd 2: Ch 1, do **not** turn; sc in each sc around, working 3 sc in center sc of each corner; join with slip st to first sc.

Rnd 3: Ch 1, 🎥 work reverse sc in each sc around (*Figs. 5a-d, page 31*); join with slip st to first st, finish off.

CHEVRONS & DIAMONDS

 INTERMEDIATE

Finished Size:

33" x 43" (84 cm x 109 cm)

SHOPPING LIST

Yarn (Medium Weight)

[4 ounces, 200 yards
(114 grams, 182 meters) per skein]:

☐ 10 skeins

Crochet Hook

☐ Size H (5 mm)

or size needed for gauge

Additional Supplies

☐ Yarn needle

GAUGE INFORMATION

16 sc = 4" (10 cm) and

22 rows = 6" (15 cm)

Gauge Swatch: 4" x 6" (10 cm x 15 cm)

Ch 17.

Row 1: Sc in second ch from hook and in each ch across: 16 sc.

Rows 2-22: Ch 1, turn; sc in each sc across.

Finish off.

STITCH GUIDE

FRONT POST CLUSTER
(abbreviated FP Cluster)

YO, insert hook from **front** to **back** around post of st indicated *(Fig. 3, page 31)*, YO and pull up a loop even with loops on hook, YO and draw through 2 loops on hook, YO, insert hook from **front** to **back** around **same** st, YO and pull up a loop even with loops on hook, YO and draw through 2 loops on hook, YO and draw through all 3 loops on hook. Skip st behind FP Cluster.

FRONT POST JOINING CLUSTER
(abbreviated FP Joining Cluster)

YO, insert hook from **front** to **back** around post of first FP Cluster 2 rows **below**, YO and pull up a loop even with loops on hook, YO and draw through 2 loops on hook, YO, insert hook from **front** to **back** around **same** st, YO and pull up a loop even with loops on hook, YO and draw through 2 loops on hook, YO, insert hook from **front** to **back** around post of next FP Cluster 2 rows **below**, YO and pull up a loop even with loops on hook, YO and draw through 2 loops on hook, YO, insert hook from **front** to **back** around **same** st, YO and pull up a loop even with loops on hook, YO and draw through 2 loops on hook, YO and draw through all 5 loops on hook. Skip st behind st just made.

SINGLE CROCHET DECREASE
(abbreviated sc decrease)

(Insert hook in **next** st or sp, YO and pull up a loop) twice, YO and draw through all 3 loops on hook (**counts as one sc**).

INSTRUCTIONS
BEGINNING SECTION

Ch 2.

Row 1 (Right side)**:** 2 Sc in second ch from hook.

Note: Loop a short piece of yarn around any stitch on Row 1 to mark **right** side.

Row 2: Ch 1, turn; 2 sc in each sc across: 4 sc.

Rows 3 and 4 (Increase rows)**:** Ch 1, turn; 2 sc in first st, sc in each st across to last st, 2 sc in last st: 8 sc.

Row 5: Ch 1, turn; 2 sc in first sc, sc in next sc, skip first 2 sc 2 rows **below** and FP Cluster around next sc, sc in next 2 sc, FP Cluster around **same** sc as previous FP Cluster, sc in next sc, 2 sc in last sc: 10 sts.

Row 6: Repeat Row 3: 12 sc.

Row 7: Ch 1, turn; 2 sc in first sc, sc in next 2 sc, FP Cluster around first FP Cluster **below**, sc in next 4 sts, FP Cluster around next FP Cluster **below**, sc in next 2 sc, 2 sc in last sc: 14 sts.

Row 8: Repeat Row 3: 16 sc.

Row 9: Ch 1, turn; 2 sc in first sc, sc in next 2 sc, FP Cluster around first FP Cluster **below**, sc in next 8 sc, FP Cluster around next FP Cluster **below**, sc in next 2 sc, 2 sc in last sc: 18 sts.

Row 10: Repeat Row 3: 20 sc.

Row 11: Ch 1, turn; 2 sc in first sc, sc in next 6 sc, FP Cluster around first FP Cluster **below**, sc in next 4 sc, FP Cluster around next FP Cluster **below**, sc in next 6 sc, 2 sc in last sc: 22 sts.

Row 12: Repeat Row 3: 24 sc.

Row 13: Ch 1, turn; 2 sc in first sc, sc in next 9 sc, FP Cluster around first FP Cluster **below**, sc in next 2 sc, FP Cluster around next FP Cluster **below**, sc in next 9 sc, 2 sc in last sc: 26 sts.

Row 14: Repeat Row 3: 28 sc.

Row 15: Ch 1, turn; 2 sc in first sc, sc in next 12 sc, work FP Joining Cluster, sc in next 13 sc, 2 sc in last sc: 30 sts.

Rows 16-18: Repeat Row 3, 3 times: 36 sc.

Row 19 (High Ridge Front - first row)**:** Ch 1, turn; ▥ sc in Front Loop Only of each sc across (*Fig. 1, page 31*).

Row 20 (High Ridge Front - second row)**:** Ch 1, turn; ▥ working in free loops of sc in row **below** (*Fig. 2, page 31*), 2 sc in first sc, sc in each st across to last st, 2 sc in last st: 38 sc.

Row 21: Ch 1, turn; 2 sc in first sc, sc in next sc, ch 3, skip next 2 sc, sc in next sc, **turn**; sc in each ch of ch-3 just made, slip st in next sc (at beginning of ch-3), **turn**; working **behind** ch-3, sc in 2 skipped sc, ★ ch 3, skip sc at end of Cable and next 2 sc, sc in next sc, **turn**; sc in each ch of ch-3 just made, slip st in next sc, **turn**; working **behind** ch-3, sc in 2 skipped sc; repeat from ★ across to last 3 sc, ch 1, sc in **same** st as last sc: 12 Cables.

Row 22: Ch 1, turn; 2 sc in first sc, skip next ch-1 sp, ★ working in **front** of Cables, 2 sc in next sc, sc in next sc, skip next sc (beginning of Cable); repeat from ★ across to last 2 sc, 2 sc in each of last 2 sc: 42 sc.

Rows 23 and 24: Repeat Rows 19 and 20: 44 sc.

Rows 25 and 26: Repeat Row 3 twice: 48 sc.

Row 27: Ch 1, turn; 2 sc in first sc, sc in next 2 sc, FP Cluster around first sc 2 rows **below**, ★ sc in next 5 sc, skip next 5 sc 2 rows **below**, FP Cluster around next sc; repeat from ★ across to last 2 sc, sc in next sc, 2 sc in last sc: 50 sts.

Row 28: Repeat Row 3: 52 sc.

Row 29: Ch 1, turn; 2 sc in first sc, sc in next 6 sc, FP Cluster around first FP Cluster **below**, ★ sc in next 5 sc, FP Cluster around next FP Cluster **below**; repeat from ★ across to last 2 sc, sc in next sc, 2 sc in last sc: 54 sts.

Row 30: Repeat Row 3: 56 sc.

Row 31: Ch 1, turn; 2 sc in first sc, sc in next 6 sc, FP Cluster around first FP Cluster **below**, ★ sc in next 5 sc, FP Cluster around next FP Cluster **below**; repeat from ★ across to last 6 sc, sc in next 5 sc, 2 sc in last sc: 58 sts.

Row 32: Repeat Row 3: 60 sc.

Row 33: Ch 1, turn; 2 sc in first sc, sc in next 7 sc, FP Cluster around first FP Cluster **below**, ★ sc in next 5 sc, FP Cluster around next FP Cluster **below**; repeat from ★ across to last 9 sc, sc in next 8 sc, 2 sc in last sc: 62 sts.

Rows 34-36: Repeat Row 3, 3 times: 68 sc.

Rows 37 and 38: Repeat Rows 19 and 20: 70 sc.

Row 39: Ch 1, turn; 2 sc in first sc, ch 3, skip next 2 sc, sc in next sc, **turn**; sc in each ch of ch-3 just made, slip st in next sc (at beginning of ch-3), **turn**; working **behind** ch-3, sc in 2 skipped sc, ★ ch 3, skip sc at end of Cable and next 2 sc, sc in next sc, **turn**; sc in each ch of ch-3 just made, slip st in next sc, **turn**; working **behind** ch-3, sc in 2 skipped sc; repeat from ★ across, ch 1, sc in same st as last sc: 23 Cables.

Row 40: Ch 1, turn; 2 sc in first sc, skip next ch-1 sp, ★ working in **front** of Cables, 2 sc in next sc, sc in next sc, skip next sc (beginning of Cable); repeat from ★ across to last 2 sc, sc in next sc, 2 sc in last sc: 74 sc.

Rows 41 and 42: Repeat Rows 19 and 20: 76 sc.

Rows 43 and 44: Repeat Row 3 twice: 80 sc.

Row 45: Ch 1, turn; 2 sc in first sc, sc in next 2 sc, FP Cluster around fourth sc 2 rows **below**, ★ sc in next 2 sc, FP Cluster around **same** st as previous FP Cluster, sc in next 10 sc, skip next 13 sc 2 rows **below**, FP Cluster around next sc; repeat from ★ 4 times **more**, sc in next 2 sc, FP Cluster around **same** st as previous FP Cluster, sc in next 2 sc, 2 sc in last sc: 82 sts.

Row 46: Repeat Row 3: 84 sc.

Row 47: Ch 1, turn; 2 sc in first sc, sc in next 3 sc, ★ † FP Cluster around next FP Cluster **below**, sc in next 4 sc, FP Cluster around next FP Cluster **below** †, sc in next 8 sc; repeat from ★ 4 times **more**, then repeat from † to † once, sc in next 3 sc , 2 sc in last sc: 86 sc.

Row 48: Repeat Row 3: 88 sc.

Row 49: Ch 1, turn; 2 sc in first sc, sc in next 3 sc, ★ † FP Cluster around next FP Cluster **below**, sc in next 8 sc, FP Cluster around next FP Cluster **below** †, sc in next 4 sc; repeat from ★ 4 times **more**, then repeat from † to † once, sc in next 3 sc, 2 sc in last sc: 90 sts.

Row 50: Repeat Row 3: 92 sc.

Row 51: Ch 1, turn; 2 sc in first sc, sc in next 7 sc, ★ † FP Cluster around next FP Cluster **below**, sc in next 4 sc, FP Cluster around next FP Cluster **below** †, sc in next 8 sc; repeat from ★ 4 times **more**, then repeat from † to † once, sc in next 7 sc, 2 sc in last sc: 94 sc.

Row 52: Repeat Row 3: 96 sc.

Row 53: Ch 1, turn; 2 sc in first sc, sc in next 10 sc, ★ † FP Cluster around next FP Cluster **below**, sc in next 2 sc, FP Cluster around next FP Cluster **below** †, sc in next 10 sc; repeat from ★ 4 times **more**, then repeat from † to † once, sc in next 10 sc , 2 sc in last sc: 98 sc.

Row 54: Repeat Row 3: 100 sc.

Row 55: Ch 1, turn; 2 sc in first sc, ★ sc in next 13 sc, work FP Joining Cluster; repeat from ★ 5 times **more**, sc in next 14 sc, 2 sc in last sc: 102 sts.

Rows 56-58: Repeat Row 3, 3 times: 108 sc.

Rows 59-64: Repeat Rows 19-24: 36 Cables on Row 61; 116 sc on Row 64.

Rows 65-76: Repeat Rows 25-36: 140 sc.

Rows 77-82: Repeat Rows 37-42: 47 Cables on Row 79; 148 sc on Row 82.

Rows 83 and 84: Repeat Row 3 twice: 152 sc.

Row 85: Ch 1, turn; 2 sc in first sc, sc in next 3 sc, FP Cluster around fifth sc 2 rows **below**, ★ sc in next 2 sc, FP Cluster around **same** st as previous FP Cluster, sc in next 10 sc, skip next 13 sc 2 rows **below** and FP Cluster around next sc; repeat from ★ 9 times **more**, sc in next 2 sc, FP Cluster around **same** st as previous FP Cluster, sc in next 3 sc, 2 sc in last sc: 154 sts.

Row 86: Repeat Row 3: 156 sc.

Row 87: Ch 1, turn; 2 sc in first sc, sc in next 4 sc, ★ † FP Cluster around next FP Cluster **below**, sc in next 4 sc, FP Cluster around next FP Cluster **below** †, sc in next 8 sc; repeat from ★ 9 times **more**, then repeat from † to † once, sc in next 4 sc , 2 sc in last sc: 158 sts.

Row 88: Repeat Row 3: 160 sc.

Row 89: Ch 1, turn; 2 sc in first sc, sc in next 4 sc, ★ FP Cluster around next FP Cluster **below**, sc in next 8 sc, FP Cluster around next FP Cluster **below**, sc in next 4 sc; repeat from ★ 10 times **more**, 2 sc in last st: 162 sts.

Row 90: Repeat Row 3: 164 sc.

Row 91: Ch 1, turn; 2 sc in first sc, sc in next 8 sc, ★ FP Cluster around next FP Cluster **below**, sc in next 4 sc, FP Cluster around next FP Cluster **below**, sc in next 8 sc; repeat from ★ 10 times **more**, 2 sc in last sc: 166 sts.

Row 92: Repeat Row 3: 168 sc.

Row 93: Ch 1, turn; 2 sc in first sc, sc in next 11 sc, ★ † FP Cluster around next FP Cluster **below**, sc in next 2 sc, FP Cluster around next FP Cluster **below** †, sc in next 10 sc; repeat from ★ 9 times **more**, then repeat from † to † once, sc in next 11 sts, 2 sc in last st: 170 sts.

Row 94: Repeat Row 3: 172 sc.

Row 95: Ch 1, turn; 2 sc in first sc, sc in next 14 sc, work FP Joining Cluster, ★ sc in next 13 sc, work FP Joining Cluster; repeat from ★ 9 times **more**, sc in next 15 sc, 2 sc in last sc: 174 sts.

CENTER SECTION

Stitch count remains constant at 174 sts through Row 128.

Row 96: Ch 1, turn; sc decrease, sc in each st across to last sc, 2 sc in last sc.

Row 97: Ch 1, turn; 2 sc in first sc, sc in each sc across to last 2 sc, sc decrease.

Row 98: Repeat Row 96.

Row 99: Ch 1, turn; sc in Front Loop Only of each sc across.

Row 100: Ch 1, turn; working in free loops of sc in row **below**, sc decrease, sc in each sc across to last st, 2 sc in last st.

Row 101: Ch 1, turn; 2 sc in first sc, ★ ch 3, skip next 2 sc, sc in next sc, **turn**; sc in each ch of ch-3 just made, slip st in next sc (at beginning of ch-3), **turn**; working **behind** ch-3, sc in 2 skipped sc; repeat from ★ across to last 2 sc, ch 1, sc decrease: 57 Cables.

Row 102: Ch 1, turn; sc in first sc, skip next ch-1 sp, ★ working in **front** of Cables, 2 sc in next sc, sc in next sc, skip next sc (beginning of Cable); repeat from ★ across to last sc, 2 sc in last sc.

Rows 103 and 104: Repeat Rows 99 and 100.

Rows 105-108: Repeat Rows 97 and 98 twice.

Row 109: Ch 1, turn; 2 sc in first sc, sc in next 2 sc, FP Cluster around first sc 2 rows **below**, ★ sc in next 5 sc, skip next 5 sc 2 rows **below**, FP Cluster around next sc; repeat from ★ across to last 8 sc, sc in next 6 sc, sc decrease.

Row 110: Repeat Row 96.

Row 111: Ch 1, turn; 2 sc in first sc, sc in next 6 sc, FP Cluster around first FP Cluster **below**, ★ sc in next 5 sc, FP Cluster around next FP Cluster **below**; repeat from ★ across to last 4 sc, sc in next 2 sc, sc decrease.

Row 112: Repeat Row 96.

Row 113: Ch 1, turn; 2 sc in first sc, sc in next 6 sc, ★ FP Cluster around next FP Cluster **below**, sc in next 5 sc; repeat from ★ across to last 4 sc, sc in next 2 sc, sc decrease.

Row 114: Repeat Row 96.

Row 115: Ch 1, turn; 2 sc in first sc, sc in next 7 sc, FP Cluster around next FP Cluster **below**, ★ sc in next 5 sc, FP Cluster around next FP Cluster **below**; repeat from ★ across to last 3 sc, sc in next sc, sc decrease.

Rows 116-120: Repeat Rows 96 and 97 twice, then repeat Row 96 once **more**.

Rows 121-126: Repeat Rows 99-104.

Row 127: Repeat Row 97.

Row 128: Repeat Row 96.

END SECTION

Row 129: Ch 1, turn; sc decrease, sc in next 13 sc, FP Cluster around 16th sc 2 rows **below**, ★ sc in next 2 sc, FP Cluster around **same** st as previous FP Cluster, sc in next 10 sc, skip next 13 sc 2 rows **below** and work FP Cluster around next sc; repeat from ★ 9 times **more**, sc in next 2 sc, FP Cluster around **same** st as previous FP Cluster, sc in next 13 sc, sc decrease: 172 sts.

Row 130 (Decrease row)**:** Ch 1, turn; sc decrease, sc in each st across to last 2 sc, sc decrease: 170 sc.

Row 131: Ch 1, turn; sc decrease, sc in next 10 sc, ★ † FP Cluster around next FP Cluster **below**, sc in next 4 sc, FP Cluster around next FP Cluster **below** †, sc in next 8 sc; repeat from ★ 9 times **more**, then repeat from † to † once, sc in next 10 sc, sc decrease: 168 sts.

Row 132: Repeat Row 130: 166 sc.

Row 133: Ch 1, turn; sc decrease, sc in next 6 sc, ★ † FP Cluster around next FP Cluster **below**, sc in next 8 sc, FP Cluster around next FP Cluster **below** †, sc in next 4 sc; repeat from ★ 9 times **more**, then repeat from † to † once, sc in next 6 sc , sc decrease: 164 sts.

Row 134: Repeat Row 130: 162 sc.

Row 135: Ch 1, turn; sc decrease, sc in next 6 sc, ★ † FP Cluster around next FP Cluster **below**, sc in next 4 sc, FP Cluster around next FP Cluster **below** †, sc in next 8 sts; repeat from ★ 9 times **more**, then repeat from † to † once, sc in next 6 sc , sc decrease: 160 sc.

Row 136: Repeat Row 130: 158 sc.

Row 137: Ch 1, turn; sc decrease, sc in next 5 sc, ★ † FP Cluster around next FP Cluster **below**, sc in next 2 sc, FP Cluster around next FP Cluster **below** †, sc in next 10 sts; repeat from ★ 9 times **more**, then repeat from † to † once, sc in next 5 sc, sc decrease: 156 sts.

Row 138: Repeat Row 130: 154 sc.

Row 139: Ch 1, turn; sc decrease, sc in next 5 sc, work FP Joining Cluster, ★ sc in next 13 sc, work FP Joining Cluster; repeat from ★ 9 times **more**, sc in next 4 sc, sc decrease: 152 sc.

Rows 140-142: Repeat Row 130, 3 times: 146 sc.

Row 143: Ch 1, turn; sc in Front Loop Only of each sc across.

Row 144: Ch 1, turn; working in free loops of sc in row **below**, sc decrease, sc in each sc across to last 2 sc, sc decrease: 144 sc.

Row 145: Ch 1, turn; sc decrease, sc in next sc, ★ ch 3, skip next 2 sc, sc in next sc, **turn**; sc in each ch of ch-3 just made, slip st in next sc (at beginning of ch-3), **turn**; working **behind** ch-3, sc in 2 skipped sc; repeat from ★ across to last 3 sc, ch 1, sc in next sc, sc decrease: 46 Cables.

Row 146: Ch 1, turn; sc decrease, skip next ch-1 sp, working in **front** of Cables, ★ 2 sc in next sc, sc in next sc, skip next sc (beginning of Cable); repeat from ★ across to last 2 sc, sc decrease: 140 sc

Rows 147 and 148: Repeat Rows 143 and 144: 138 sc.

Rows 149 and 150: Repeat Row 130 twice: 134 sc.

Row 151: Ch 1, turn; sc decrease, sc in next 11 sc, FP Cluster around 13th sc 2 rows **below**, ★ sc in next 5 sc, skip next 5 sc 2 rows **below** and FP Cluster around next sc; repeat from ★ across to last 12 sc, sc in next 10 sc, sc decrease: 132 sts.

Row 152: Repeat Row 130: 130 sc.

Row 153: Ch 1, turn; sc decrease, sc in next 11 sc, FP Cluster around first FP Cluster **below**, ★ sc in next 5 sc, FP Cluster around next FP Cluster **below**; repeat from ★ across to last 8 sc, sc in next 6 sc, sc decrease: 128 sts.

Row 154: Repeat Row 130: 126 sc.

Row 155: Ch 1, turn; sc decrease, sc in next 7 sc, FP Cluster around next FP Cluster **below**, ★ sc in next 5 sc, FP Cluster around next FP Cluster **below**; repeat from ★ across to last 8 sc, sc in next 6 sc, sc decrease: 124 sts.

Row 156: Repeat Row 130: 122 sc.

Row 157: Ch 1, turn; sc decrease, sc in next 4 sc, ★ FP Cluster around next FP Cluster **below**, sc in next 5 sc; repeat from ★ across to last 2 sc, sc decrease: 120 sts.

Rows 158-160: Repeat Row 130, 3 times: 114 sc.

Rows 161 and 162: Repeat Rows 143 and 144: 112 sc.

Row 163: Ch 1, turn; sc decrease, ★ ch 3, skip next 2 sc, sc in next sc, **turn**; sc in each ch of ch-3 just made, slip st in next sc (at beginning of ch-3), **turn**; working **behind** ch-3, sc in 2 skipped sc; repeat from ★ across to last 2 sc, ch 1, sc decrease: 36 Cables.

Row 164: Ch 1, turn; sc in first sc, skip next ch-1 sp, working in **front** of Cables, sc in next 2 sc, skip next sc (beginning of Cable), ★ 2 sc in next sc, sc in next sc, skip next sc (beginning of Cable); repeat from ★ across to last Cable, sc in next 2 sc and in last sc: 108 sc.

Rows 165 and 166: Repeat Rows 143 and 144: 106 sc.

Rows 167 and 168: Repeat Row 130 twice: 102 sc.

Row 169: Ch 1, turn; sc decrease, sc in next 12 sc, FP Cluster around 17th 2 rows **below**, ★ sc in next 2 sc, FP Cluster around **same** st as previous FP Cluster, sc in next 10 sc, skip next 13 sc 2 rows **below** and FP Cluster around next sc; repeat from ★ 4 times **more**, sc in next 2 sc, FP Cluster around **same** st as previous FP Cluster, sc in next 12 sc, sc decrease: 100 sts.

Row 170: Repeat Row 130: 98 sc.

Row 171: Ch 1, turn; sc decrease, sc in next 9 sc, ★ † FP Cluster around next FP Cluster **below**, sc in next 4 sc, FP Cluster around next FP Cluster **below** †, sc in next 8 sc; repeat from ★ 4 times **more**, then repeat from † to † once, sc in next 9 sc, sc decrease: 96 sts.

Row 172: Repeat Row 130: 94 sc.

Row 173: Ch 1, turn; sc decrease, sc in next 5 sc, ★ † FP Cluster around next FP Cluster **below**, sc in next 8 sc, FP Cluster around next FP Cluster **below** †, sc in next 4 sc; repeat from ★ 4 times **more**, then repeat from † to † once, sc in next 5 sc, sc decrease: 92 sts.

Row 174: Repeat Row 130: 90 sc.

Row 175: Ch 1, turn; sc decrease, sc in next 5 sc, ★ † FP Cluster around next FP Cluster **below**, sc in next 4 sc, FP Cluster around next FP Cluster **below** †, sc in next 8 sc; repeat from ★ 4 times **more**, then repeat from † to † once, sc in next 5 sc , sc decrease: 88 sc.

Row 176: Repeat Row 130: 86 sc.

Row 177: Ch 1, turn; sc decrease, sc in next 4 sc, ★ † FP Cluster around next FP Cluster **below**, sc in next 2 sc, FP Cluster around next FP Cluster **below** †, sc in next 10 sts; repeat from ★ 4 times **more**, then repeat from † to † once, sc in next 4 sc, sc decrease: 84 sts.

Row 178: Repeat Row 130: 82 sc.

Row 179: Ch 1, turn; sc decrease, sc in next 3 sc, work FP Joining Cluster, ★ sc in next 13 sc, work FP Joining Cluster; repeat from ★ 4 times **more**, sc in next 4 sc, sc decrease: 80 sc.

Rows 180-182: Repeat Row 130, 3 times: 74 sc.

Rows 183-188: Repeat Rows 143-148: 22 Cables on Row 185, 66 sc on Row 188.

Rows 189 and 190: Repeat Row 130 twice: 62 sc.

Rows 191-197: Repeat Rows 151-157: 48 sc.

Rows 198-200: Repeat Row 130, 3 times: 42 sc.

Rows 201-206: Repeat Rows 161-166: 12 Cables on Row 203, 34 sc on Row 206.

Rows 207 and 208: Repeat Row 130 twice: 30 sc.

Row 209: Ch 1, turn; sc decrease, sc in next 11 sc, skip first 15 sc 2 rows **below** and FP Cluster around next sc, sc in next 2 sc, FP Cluster around **same** sc as previous FP Cluster, sc in next 11 sc, sc decrease: 28 sts.

Row 210: Repeat Row 130: 26 sc.

Row 211: Ch 1, turn; sc decrease, sc in next 8 sc, FP Cluster around first FP Cluster **below**, sc in next 4 sc, FP Cluster around next FP Cluster **below**, sc in next 8 sc, sc decrease: 24 sts.

Row 212: Repeat Row 130: 22 sc.

Row 213: Ch 1, turn; sc decrease, sc in next 4 sc, FP Cluster around first FP Cluster **below**, sc in next 8 sc, FP Cluster around next FP Cluster **below**, sc in next 4 sc, sc decrease: 20 sts.

Row 214: Repeat Row 130: 18 sc.

Row 215: Ch 1, turn; sc decrease, sc in next 4 sc, FP Cluster around first FP Cluster **below**, sc in next 4 sc, FP Cluster around next FP Cluster **below**, sc in next 4 sc, sc decrease: 16 sts.

Row 216: Repeat Row 130: 14 sc.

Row 217: Ch 1, turn; sc decrease, sc in next 3 sc, FP Cluster around first FP Cluster **below**, sc in next 2 sc, FP Cluster around next FP Cluster **below**, sc in next 3 sc, sc decrease: 12 sts.

Row 218: Repeat Row 130: 10 sc.

Row 219: Ch 1, turn; sc decrease, sc in next 2 sc, work FP Joining Cluster, sc in next 3 sc, sc decrease: 8 sts.

Rows 220 and 221: Repeat Row 130 twice: 4 sc.

Row 222: Ch 1, turn; sc decrease twice: 2 sc.

Row 223: Ch 1, turn; sc decrease; do **not** finish off.

BORDER

Rnd 1: Ch 1, do **not** turn: 🎥 sc evenly around, working 3 sc in each corner; join with slip st to first sc.

Rnd 2: Ch 1, 🎥 work reverse sc in each sc around *(Figs. 5a-d, page 31)*; join with slip st to first st, finish off.

POPCORN DIAMONDS

 **INTERMEDIATE**

Finished Size:

35" x 45" (89 cm x 114 cm)

SHOPPING LIST

Yarn (Medium Weight)

[4 ounces, 186 yards
(113 grams, 170 meters) per skein]:

☐ 12 skeins

Crochet Hooks

☐ Size H (5 mm) **and**

☐ Size J (6 mm)

   or sizes needed for gauge

Additional Supplies

☐ Yarn needle

GAUGE INFORMATION

With smaller size hook,

   16 sc = 4" (10 cm)

   and 28 rows = 6" (15 cm)

Gauge Swatch: 4" x 6" (10 cm x 15 cm)
Ch 17.

Row 1: Sc in second ch from hook and
in each ch across: 16 sc.

Rows 2-28: Ch 1, turn; sc in each sc
across.
Finish off.

STITCH GUIDE

🎥 FRONT POST CLUSTER
   (abbreviated FP Cluster)

YO, insert hook from **front** to **back**
around post of st indicated *(Fig. 3,
page 31)*, YO and pull up a loop even
with loop on hook, YO and draw
through 2 loops on hook, YO, insert
hook from **front** to **back** around **same**
st, YO and pull up a loop even with
loop on hook, YO and draw through
2 loops on hook, YO and draw through
all 3 loops on hook. Skip st behind
FP Cluster.

🎥 SINGLE CROCHET DECREASE
   (abbreviated sc decrease)

(Insert hook in **next** st or sp, YO and
pull up a loop) twice, YO and draw
through all 3 loops on hook (**counts as
one sc**).

🎥 SMALL POPCORN
   (uses one st or sp)

(Sc, 2 hdc, sc) in st indicated, drop loop
from hook, insert hook in first sc of 4-st
group, hook dropped loop and draw
through *(Fig. 4, page 31)*, ch 1 to close.

🎥 LARGE POPCORN
   (uses one st or sp)

Work 4 dc in st indicated, drop loop
from hook, insert hook in first dc of
4-dc group, hook dropped loop and
draw through *(Fig. 4, page 31)*, ch 1 to
close.

INSTRUCTIONS
BEGINNING SECTION

With larger size hook, ch 2.

Row 1 (Right side)**:** 3 Sc in second ch
from hook.

Note: Loop a short piece of yarn
around any stitch on Row 1 to mark
right side.

Row 2: Ch 1, turn; 2 sc in first st, sc in
next sc, 2 sc in last st: 5 sc.

Row 3: Ch 1, turn; 2 sc in first sc, ch 1,
skip next sc, work Small Popcorn in
next sc, ch 1, skip next sc, 2 sc in last sc:
4 sc, 1 Small Popcorn, and 2 ch-1 sps.

Row 4: Ch 1, turn; working loosely, 2 sc
in first sc, ★ ch 1, skip next st, sc in next
ch-1 sp; repeat from ★ once **more**,
ch 1, skip next sc, 2 sc in last sc:
6 sc and 3 ch-1 sps.

Row 5: Ch 1, turn; 2 sc in first sc, ch 1, skip next sc, work Small Popcorn in next ch-1 sp, ch 1, skip next sc, sc in next ch-1 sp, ch 1, skip next sc, work Small Popcorn in next ch-1 sp, ch 1, skip next sc, 2 sc in last sc: 5 sc, 2 Small Popcorns, and 4 ch-1 sps.

Row 6: Ch 1, turn; working loosely, 2 sc in first sc, ★ ch 1, skip next st, sc in next ch-1 sp; repeat from ★ across to last 2 sc, ch 1, skip next sc, 2 sc in last sc: 8 sc and 5 ch-1 sps.

Row 7: Ch 1, turn; 2 sc in first sc, ch 1, skip next sc, work Small Popcorn in next ch-1 sp, ★ ch 1, skip next sc, sc in next ch-1 sp, ch 1, skip next sc, work Small Popcorn in next ch-1 sp; repeat from ★ across to last 2 sc, ch 1, skip next sc, 2 sc in last sc: 6 sc, 3 Small Popcorns, and 6 ch-1 sps.

Rows 8-15: Repeat Rows 6 and 7, 4 times: 10 sc, 7 Small Popcorns and 14 ch-1 sps.

Row 16: Ch 1, turn; 2 sc in first sc, sc in next sc, 2 sc in each ch-1 sp across to last 2 sc, skip next sc, 2 sc in last sc: 33 sc.

Change to smaller size hook.

Row 17 (High Ridge Front - first row): Ch 1, turn; 🎥 sc in Front Loop Only of each sc across (*Fig. 1, page 31*).

Row 18 (High Ridge Front - second row): Ch 1, turn; 🎥 working in free loops of sc in row below (*Fig. 2, page 31*), 2 sc in first sc, sc in each st across to last st, 2 sc in last st: 35 sc.

Rows 19-22 (Increase rows): Ch 1, turn; 2 sc in first st, sc in each st across to last st, 2 sc in last st: 43 sc.

Row 23: Ch 1, turn; 2 sc in first sc, sc in next 6 sc, (work Large Popcorn in next sc, sc in next 13 sc) twice, work Large Popcorn in next sc, sc in next 6 sc, 2 sc in last sc: 45 sts.

Row 24: Repeat Row 19: 47 sc.

Row 25: Ch 1, turn; 2 sc in first sc, sc in next 6 sc, (work Large Popcorn in next sc, sc in next 3 sc, work Large Popcorn in next sc, sc in next 9 sc) twice, work Large Popcorn in next sc, sc in next 3 sc, work Large Popcorn in next sc, sc in next 6 sc, 2 sc in last sc: 49 sts.

Row 26: Repeat Row 19: 51 sc.

Row 27: Ch 1, turn; 2 sc in first sc, sc in next 6 sc, (work Large Popcorn in next sc, sc in next 7 sc, work Large Popcorn in next sc, sc in next 5 sc) twice, work Large Popcorn in next sc, sc in next 7 sc, work Large Popcorn in next sc, sc in next 6 sc, 2 sc in last sc: 53 sc.

Row 28: Repeat Row 19: 55 sc.

Row 29: Ch 1, turn; 2 sc in first sc, sc in next 10 sc, (work Large Popcorn in next sc, sc in next 3 sc, work Large Popcorn in next sc, sc in next 9 sc) twice, work Large Popcorn in next sc, sc in next 3 sc, work Large Popcorn in next sc, sc in next 10 sc, 2 sc in last sc: 57 sc.

Row 30: Repeat Row 19: 59 sc.

Row 31: Ch 1, turn; 2 sc in first sc, sc in next 14 sc, (work Large Popcorn in next sc, sc in next 13 sc) twice, work Large Popcorn in next sc, sc in next 14 sc, 2 sc in last sc: 61 sc.

Rows 32-36: Repeat Row 19, 5 times: 71 sc.

Rows 37 and 38: Repeat Rows 17 and 18: 73 sc.

Rows 39-42: Repeat Row 19, 4 times: 81 sc.

Row 43: Ch 1, turn; 2 sc in first sc, sc in next 4 sc, skip first 3 sc 2 rows **below** and FP Cluster around next sc, ★ sc in next 6 sc, skip next 6 sc 2 rows **below** and FP Cluster around next sc; repeat from ★ across to last 5 sc, sc in next 4 sc, 2 sc in last sc: 83 sts.

Row 44: Repeat Row 19: 85 sc.

Row 45: Ch 1, turn; 2 sc in first sc, sc in next sc, FP Cluster around first sc rows **below**, ★ sc in next 6 sc, FP Cluster around next FP Cluster below; repeat from ★ across to last sc, sc in next 4 sc, 2 sc in last sc: 7 sts.

Row 46: Repeat Row 19: 89 sc.

Row 47: Ch 1, turn; 2 sc in first sc, sc in next 5 sc, FP Cluster around first FP Cluster **below**, ★ sc in next 6 sc, FP Cluster around next FP Cluster below; repeat from ★ across to last sc, sc in next 4 sc, 2 sc in last sc: 91 sts.

Row 48: Repeat Row 19: 93 sc.

Row 49: Ch 1, turn; 2 sc in first sc, sc in next 2 sc, FP Cluster around first sc rows **below**, ★ sc in next 6 sc, FP Cluster around next FP Cluster below; repeat from ★ across to last sc, sc in next 4 sc, 2 sc in last sc: 95 sts.

Row 50: Repeat Row 19: 97 sc.

Row 51: Ch 1, turn; 2 sc in first sc, ★ sc in next 6 sc, FP Cluster around next FP Cluster **below**; repeat from ★ across to last 5 sc, sc in next 4 sc, 2 sc in last sc: 99 sts.

Rows 52-54: Repeat Row 19, 3 times: 105 sc.

Rows 55 and 56: Repeat Rows 17 and 18: 107 sc.

Change to larger size hook.

Row 57: Ch 1, turn; 2 sc in first sc, ★ ch 1, skip next sc, work Small Popcorn in next sc, ch 1, skip next sc, sc in next sc; repeat from ★ across to last 2 sc, ch 1, skip next sc, 2 sc in last sc: 30 sc, 26 Small Popcorns, and 53 ch-1 sps.

Row 58: Repeat Row 6: 57 sc and 54 ch-1 sps.

Rows 59-69: Repeat Rows 57 and 58, 5 times; then repeat Row 57 once **more**: 36 sc, 32 Small Popcorns, and 65 ch-1 sps.

Row 70: Repeat Row 16: 135 sc.

Change to smaller size hook.

Rows 71 and 72: Repeat Rows 17 and 18: 137 sc.

Rows 73-76: Repeat Row 19, 4 times: 145 sc.

Row 77: Ch 1, turn; 2 sc in first sc, sc in next sc, ★ work Large Popcorn in next sc, sc in next 13 sc; repeat from ★ across to last 3 sc, work Large Popcorn in next sc, sc in next sc, 2 sc in last sc: 147 sts.

Row 78: Repeat Row 19: 149 sc.

Row 79: Ch 1, turn; 2 sc in first sc, sc in next sc, work Large Popcorn in next sc, sc in next 3 sc, work Large Popcorn in next sc, ★ sc in next 9 sc, work Large Popcorn in next sc, sc in next 3 sc, work Large Popcorn in next sc; repeat from ★ across to last 2 sc, sc in next sc, 2 sc in last sc: 151 sts.

Row 80: Repeat Row 19: 153 sc.

Row 81: Ch 1, turn; 2 sc in first sc, sc in next sc, work Large Popcorn in next sc, sc in next 7 sc, work Large Popcorn in next sc, ★ sc in next 5 sc, work Large Popcorn in next sc, sc in next 7 sc, work Large Popcorn in next sc; repeat from ★ across to last 2 sc, sc in next sc, 2 sc in last sc: 155 sts.

Row 82: Repeat Row 19: 157 sc.

Row 83: Ch 1, turn; 2 sc in first sc, sc in next 5 sc, work Large Popcorn in next sc, sc in next 3 sc, Large Popcorn in next sc, ★ sc in next 9 sc, work Large Popcorn in next sc, sc in next 3 sc, work Large Popcorn in next sc; repeat from ★ across to last 6 sc, sc in next 5 sc, 2 sc in last sc: 159 sts.

Row 84: Repeat Row 19: 161 sts.

Row 85: Ch 1, turn; 2 sc in first sc, sc in next 9 sc, work Large Popcorn in next sc, ★ sc in next 13 sc, work Large Popcorn in next sc; repeat from ★ across to last 10 sc, sc in next 9 sc, 2 sc in last sc: 163 sts.

Rows 86-90: Repeat Row 19, 5 times: 173 sc.

Rows 91 and 92: Repeat Rows 17 and 18: 175 sc.

Rows 93-96: Repeat Row 19, 4 times: 183 sc.

Row 97: Ch 1, turn; 2 sc in first sc, sc in next 4 sc, skip first 3 sc 2 rows **below** and FP Cluster around next sc, ★ sc in next 6 sc, skip next 6 sc 2 rows **below** and FP Cluster around next sc; repeat from ★ across to last 2 sc, sc in next sc, 2 sc in last sc: 185 sts.

Row 98: Repeat Row 19: 187 sc.

Row 99: Ch 1, turn; 2 sc in first sc, sc in next sc, FP Cluster around first sc 2 rows **below**, ★ sc in next 6 sc, FP Cluster around next FP Cluster **below**; repeat from ★ across to last 2 sc, sc in next sc, 2 sc in last sc: 189 sts.

Row 100: Repeat Row 19: 191 sc.

CENTER SECTION

Stitch count remains constant at 191 sts through Row 138.

Row 101: Ch 1, turn; 2 sc in first sc, sc in next 5 sc, FP Cluster around next FP Cluster **below**, ★ sc in next 6 sc, FP Cluster around next FP Cluster **below**; repeat from ★ across to last 2 sc, sc decrease.

Row 102: Ch 1, turn; sc decrease, sc in each st across to last st, 2 sc in last sc.

Row 103: Ch 1, turn; 2 sc in first sc, sc in next 2 sc, FP Cluster around first sc 2 rows **below**, ★ sc in next 6 sc, FP Cluster around next FP Cluster **below**; repeat from ★ across to last 5 sc, sc in next 3 sc, sc decrease.

Row 104: Repeat Row 102.

Row 105: Ch 1, turn; 2 sc in first sc, ★ sc in next 6 sc, FP Cluster around next FP Cluster **below**; repeat from ★ across to last 8 sc, sc in next 6 sc, sc decrease.

Row 106: Repeat Row 102.

Row 107: Ch 1, turn; 2 sc in first sc, sc in each sc across to last 2 sc, sc decrease.

Row 108: Repeat Row 102.

Row 109: Ch 1, turn; sc in Front Loop Only of each sc across.

Row 110: Ch 1, turn; working in free loops of sc in row **below**, sc decrease, sc in each st across to last st, 2 sc in last st.

Change to larger size hook.

Row 111: Ch 1, turn; 2 sc in first sc, ch 1, skip next sc, work Small Popcorn in next sc, ★ ch 1, skip next sc, sc in next sc, ch 1, skip next sc, work Small Popcorn in next sc; repeat from ★ across to last 4 sc, ch 1, skip next sc, sc in next sc, sc decrease: 50 sc, 47 Small Popcorns, and 94 ch-1 sps.

Row 112: Ch 1, turn; sc decrease, sc in next ch-1 sp, ★ ch 1, skip next st, sc in next ch-1 sp; repeat from ★ across to last 2 sc, ch 1, skip next sc, 2 sc in last sc.

Row 113: Ch 1, turn; 2 sc in first sc, ch 1, skip next sc, work Small Popcorn in next ch-1 sp, ch 1, skip next sc, sc in next ch-1 sp, ★ ch 1, skip next sc, work Small Popcorn in next ch-1 sp, ch 1, skip next sc, sc in next ch-1 sp; repeat from ★ across to last 2 sc, sc decrease.

Rows 114-127: Repeat Rows 112 and 113, 7 times.

Row 128: Ch 1, turn; sc decrease, 2 sc in each ch-1 sp across to last 2 sc, skip next sc, 2 sc in last sc.

Change to smaller size hook.

Rows 129 and 130: Repeat Rows 109 and 110.

Row 131: Ch 1, turn; 2 sc in first sc, sc in each sc across to last 2 sc, sc decrease.

Row 132: Repeat Row 102.

Rows 133 and 134: Repeat Rows 131 and 132.

Rows 135-138: Repeat Rows 103-106.

END SECTION

Row 139: Ch 1, turn; sc decrease, sc in next 2 sc, skip first sc 2 rows **below** and FP Cluster around next sc, ★ sc in next 5 sc, FP Cluster around next FP Cluster **below**; repeat from ★ across to last 4 sc, sc in next 2 sc, sc decrease: 189 sts.

Row 140 (Decrease row): Ch 1, turn; sc decrease, sc in each st across to last 2 sts, sc decrease: 187 sc.

Row 141: Ch 1, turn; sc decrease, sc in next 2 sc, FP Cluster around first FP Cluster **below**, ★ sc in next 6 sc, FP Cluster around next FP Cluster **below**; repeat from ★ across to last 7 sc, sc in next 5 sc, sc decrease: 185 sts.

Row 142: Repeat Row 140: 183 sc.

Row 143: Ch 1, turn; sc decrease, sc in next 2 sc, FP Cluster around first FP Cluster **below**, ★ sc in next 6 sc, FP Cluster around FP Cluster **below**; repeat from ★ across to last 3 sc, sc in next sc, sc decrease: 181 sts.

Rows 144-146: Repeat Row 140, 3 times: 175 sc.

Row 147: Ch 1, turn; sc in Front Loop Only of each sc across.

Row 148: Ch 1, turn; working in free loops of sc in row **below**, sc decrease, sc in each sc across to last 2 sc, sc decrease: 173 sc.

Rows 149-152: Repeat Row 140, 4 times: 165 sc.

Row 153: Ch 1, turn; sc decrease, sc in next 10 sc, work Large Popcorn in next sc, ★ sc in next 13 sc, work Large Popcorn in next st; repeat from ★ across to last 12 sc, sc in next 10 sc, sc decrease: 11 Large Popcorns and 152 sc.

Row 154: Repeat Row 140: 161 sc.

Row 155: Ch 1, turn; sc decrease, sc in next 6 sc, work Large Popcorn in next sc, sc in next 3 sc, work Large Popcorn in next sc, ★ sc in next 9 sc, work Large Popcorn in next sc, sc in next 3 sc, work Large Popcorn in next sc; repeat from ★ across to last 8 sc, sc in next 6 sc, sc decrease: 159 sts.

Row 156: Repeat Row 140: 157 sc.

Row 157: Ch 1, turn; sc decrease, sc in next 2 sc, work Large Popcorn in next sc, sc in next 7 sc, work Large Popcorn in next sc, ★ sc in next 5 sc, work Large Popcorn in next sc, sc in next 7 sc, work Large Popcorn in next sc; repeat from ★ across to last 4 sc, sc in next 2 sc, sc decrease: 155 sts.

Row 158: Repeat Row 140: 153 sc.

Row 159: Ch 1, turn; sc decrease, sc in next 2 sc, work Large Popcorn in next sc, sc in next 3 sc, work Large Popcorn in next sc, ★ sc in next 9 sc, work Large Popcorn in next sc, sc in next 3 sc, work Large Popcorn in next sc; repeat from ★ across to last 4 sc, sc in next 2 sc, sc decrease: 151 sts.

Row 160: Repeat Row 140: 149 sc.

Row 161: Ch 1, turn; sc decrease, sc in next 2 sc, work Large Popcorn in next sc, ★ sc in next 13 sc, work Large Popcorn in next sc; repeat from ★ across to last 4 sc, sc in next 2 sc, sc decrease: 147 sts.

Rows 162-166: Repeat Row 140, 5 times: 137 sc.

Rows 167 and 168: Repeat Rows 147 and 148: 135 sc.

Change to larger size hook.

Row 169: Ch 1, turn; sc decrease, ch 1, skip next sc, work Small Popcorn in next sc, ★ ch 1, skip next sc, sc in next sc, ch 1, skip next sc, work Small Popcorn in next sc; repeat from ★ across to last 3 sc, ch 1, skip next sc, sc decrease: 34 sc, 33 Small Popcorns, and 66 ch-1 sps.

Row 170: Ch 1, turn; sc decrease, ★ ch 1, skip next sc, sc in next ch-1 sp; repeat from ★ across to last ch-1 sp, ch 1, skip next st, sc decrease: 66 sc and 65 ch-1 sps.

Row 171: Ch 1, turn; sc decrease, ch 1, skip next sc, work Small Popcorn in next ch-1 sp, ★ ch 1, skip next sc, sc in next ch-1 sp, ch 1, skip next sc, work Small Popcorn in next ch-1 sp; repeat from ★ across to last 2 sc, ch 1, skip next sc, sc decrease: 33 sc, 32 Small Popcorns, and 64 ch-1 sps.

Rows 172-181: Repeat Rows 170 and 171, 5 times: 28 sc, 27 Small Popcorns, and 54 ch-1 sps.

Row 182: Ch 1, turn; sc decrease, 2 sc in each ch-1 sp across to last ch-1 sp, sc in last ch-1 sp and in last sc: 107 sc.

Change to smaller size hook.

Rows 183 and 184: Repeat Rows 147 and 148: 105 sc.

Rows 185-188: Repeat Row 140, 4 times: 97 sc.

Row 189: Ch 1, turn; sc decrease, sc in next 7 sc, FP Cluster around tenth sc 2 rows **below**, ★ sc in next 6 sts, skip next 6 sc 2 rows **below** and FP Cluster around next sc; repeat from ★ across to last 10 sc, sc in next 8 sc, sc decrease: 95 sts.

Row 190: Repeat Row 140: 93 sc.

Row 191: Ch 1, turn; sc decrease, sc in next 7 sc, FP Cluster around first FP Cluster **below**, ★ sc in next 6 sc, FP Cluster around next FP Cluster **below**; repeat from ★ across to last 6 sc, sc in next 4 sc, sc decrease: 91 sts.

Row 192: Repeat Row 140: 89 sc.

Row 193: Ch 1, turn; sc decrease, sc in next 7 sc, FP Cluster around first FP Cluster **below**, ★ sc in next 6 sc, FP Cluster around FP Cluster **below**; repeat from ★ across to last 2 sc, sc decrease: 87 sts.

Row 194: Repeat Row 140: 85 sc.

Row 195: Ch 1, turn; sc decrease, FP Cluster around second sc 2 rows **below**, ★ sc in next 6 sc, FP Cluster around next FP Cluster **below**; repeat from ★ across to last 5 sc, sc in next 3 sc, sc decrease: 83 sts.

Row 196: Repeat Row 140: 81 sc.

Row 197: Ch 1, turn; sc decrease, FP Cluster around first FP Cluster 2 rows **below**, ★ sc in next 6 sts, FP Cluster around next FP Cluster **below**; repeat from ★ across to last 8 sc, sc in next 6 sc, sc decrease: 79 sts.

Rows 198-200: Repeat Row 140, 3 times: 73 sc.

Rows 201 and 202: Repeat Rows 147 and 148: 71 sc.

Rows 203-206: Repeat Row 140, 4 times: 63 sc.

Row 207: Ch 1, turn; sc decrease, sc in next 15 sc, work Large Popcorn in next sc, ★ sc in next 13 sc, work Large Popcorn in next sc; repeat from ★ across to last 17 sc, sc in next 15 sc, sc decrease: 61 sts.

Row 208: Repeat Row 140: 59 sc.

Row 209: Ch 1, turn; sc decrease, sc in next 11 sc, work Large Popcorn in next sc, sc in next 3 sc, work Large Popcorn in next sc, ★ sc in next 9 sc, work Large Popcorn in next sc, sc in next 3 sc, work Large Popcorn in next sc; repeat from ★ once **more**, sc in next 11 sc, sc decrease: 57 sts.

Row 210: Repeat Row 140: 55 sc.

Row 211: Ch 1, turn; sc decrease, sc in next 7 sc, work Large Popcorn in next sc, sc in next 7 sc, work Large Popcorn in next sc, ★ sc in next 5 sc, work Large Popcorn in next sc, sc in next 7 sc, work Large Popcorn in next sc; repeat from ★ once **more**, sc in next 7 sc, sc decrease: 53 sts.

Row 212: Repeat Row 140: 51 sc.

Row 213: Ch 1, turn; sc decrease, sc in next 7 sc, work Large Popcorn in next sc, sc in next 3 sc, work Large Popcorn in next sc, ★ sc in next 9 sc, work Large Popcorn in next sc, sc in next 3 sc, work Large Popcorn in next sc; repeat from ★ once **more**, sc in next 7 sc, sc decrease: 49 sts.

Row 214: Repeat Row 140: 47 sc.

Row 215: Ch 1, turn; sc decrease, sc in next 7 sc, work Large Popcorn in next sc, ★ sc in next 13 sc, work Large Popcorn in next sc; repeat from ★ once **more**, sc in next 7 sc, sc decrease: 45 sts.

Rows 216-220: Repeat Row 140, 5 times: 35 sc.

Rows 221 and 222: Repeat Rows 147 and 148: 33 sc.

Change to larger size hook.

Row 223: Ch 1, turn; sc decrease, ★ ch 1, skip next sc, work Small Popcorn in next sc, ch 1, skip next sc, sc in next sc; repeat from ★ across to last 3 sc, ch 1, skip next sc, sc decrease.

Row 224: Ch 1, turn; sc decrease, ★ ch 1, skip next st, sc in next ch-1 sp; repeat from ★ across to last ch-1 sp, ch 1, sc decrease: 15 sc and 14 ch-1 sps.

Row 225: Ch 1, turn; sc decrease, ★ ch 1, skip next sc, work Small Popcorn in next ch-1 sp, ch 1, skip next sc, sc in next ch-1 sp; repeat from ★ across to last 2 sc, ch 1, skip next sc, sc decrease: 14 sc and 13 ch-1 sps.

Rows 226-236: Repeat Rows 224 and 225, 5 times; then repeat Row 224 once **more**: 2 sc, 1 Small Popcorn, and 2 ch-1 sps.

Row 237: Ch 1, turn; sc decrease, sc in next st, sc decrease: 3 sc.

Row 238: Ch 1, turn; (insert hook in next st, YO and pull up a loop) 3 times, YO and draw through all 4 loops on hook; do **not** finish off.

BORDER

Rnd 1: Ch 1, turn: 📹 sc evenly around, working 3 sc in each corner; join with slip st to first sc.

Rnd 2: Ch 1, do **not** turn; sc in each sc around, working 3 sc in center sc of each corner; join with slip st to first sc.

Rnd 3: Ch 1, 📹 work reverse sc in each sc around (*Figs. 5a-d, page 31*); join with slip st to first st, finish off.

29

ABBREVIATIONS

ch(s)	chain(s)
cm	centimeters
dc	double crochet(s)
FP Cluster	Front Post Cluster
hdc	half double crochet(s)
mm	millimeters
Rnd(s)	Round(s)
sc	single crochet(s)
sp(s)	space(s)
st(s)	stitch(es)
YO	yarn over

SYMBOLS & TERMS

★ — work instructions following ★ as many **more** times as indicated in addition to the first time.

† to † — work all instructions from first † to second † **as many** times as specified.

( ) or [ ] — work enclosed instructions as many times as specified by the number immediately following **or** work all enclosed instructions in the stitch or space indicated **or** contains explanatory remarks.

colon (:) — the numbers given after a colon at the end of a row denotes the number of stitches you should have on that row.

GAUGE

Exact gauge is essential for proper size. Before beginning your afghan, make the sample swatch given in the individual instruction in the yarn and hook specified. After completing the swatch, measure it, counting your stitches and rows carefully. If your swatch is larger or smaller than specified, **make another, changing hook size to get the correct gauge.** Keep trying until you find the size hook that will give you the specified gauge.

CROCHET TERMINOLOGY	
UNITED STATES	**INTERNATIONAL**
slip stitch (slip st) =	single crochet (sc)
single crochet (sc) =	double crochet (dc)
half double crochet (hdc) =	half treble crochet (htr)
double crochet (dc) =	treble crochet(tr)
treble crochet (tr) =	double treble crochet (dtr)
double treble crochet (dtr) =	triple treble crochet (ttr)
triple treble crochet (tr tr) =	quadruple treble crochet (qtr)
skip =	miss

Yarn Weight Symbol & Names	LACE 0	SUPER FINE 1	FINE 2	LIGHT 3	MEDIUM 4	BULKY 5	SUPER BULKY 6
Type of Yarns in Category	Fingering, 10-count crochet thread	Sock, Fingering Baby	Sport, Baby	DK, Light Worsted	Worsted, Afghan, Aran	Chunky, Craft, Rug	Bulky, Roving
Crochet Gauge* Ranges in Single Crochet to 4" (10 cm)	32-42 double crochets**	21-32 sts	16-20 sts	12-17 sts	11-14 sts	8-11 sts	5-9 sts
Advised Hook Size Range	Steel*** 6,7,8 Regular hook B-1	B-1 to E-4	E-4 to 7	7 to I-9	I-9 to K-10.5	K-10.5 to M-13	M-13 and larger

*GUIDELINES ONLY: The chart above reflects the most commonly used gauges and hook sizes for specific yarn categories.

** Lace weight yarns are usually crocheted on larger-size hooks to create lacy openwork patterns. Accordingly, a gauge range is difficult to determine. Always follow the gauge stated in your pattern.

*** Steel crochet hooks are sized differently from regular hooks–the higher the number the smaller the hook, which is the reverse of regular hook sizing.

CROCHET HOOKS															
U.S.	B-1	C-2	D-3	E-4	F-5	G-6	H-8	I-9	J-10	K-10½	L-11	M/N-13	N/P-15	P/Q	Q	S
Metric - mm	2.25	2.75	3.25	3.5	3.75	4	5	5.5	6	6.5	8	9	10	15	16	19

■□□□ BEGINNER	Projects for first-time crocheters using basic stitches. Minimal shaping.
■■□□ EASY	Projects using yarn with basic stitches, repetitive stitch patterns, simple color changes, and simple shaping and finishing.
■■■□ INTERMEDIATE	Projects using a variety of techniques, such as basic lace patterns or color patterns, mid-level shaping and finishing.
■■■■ EXPERIENCED	Projects with intricate stitch patterns, techniques and dimension, such as non-repeating patterns, multi-color techniques, fine threads, small hooks, detailed shaping and refined finishing.

HINTS

...s in all crocheted pieces, good ...nishing techniques make a big ...ifference in the quality of the ...iece. Make a habit of taking care ...f loose ends as you work. Thread a ...arn needle with the yarn end. With **wrong** side facing, weave the needle ...hrough several stitches, then reverse ...he direction and weave it back ...hrough several stitches. When ends ...re secure, clip them off close to work.

BACK OR FRONT LOOPS ONLY

...Work only in loop(s) indicated by ...rrow *(Fig. 1)*.

...ig. 1

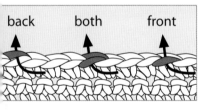

FREE LOOPS

...fter working in Back or Front Loops ...Only on a row, there will be a ridge of ...nused loops called the free loops. ...ater, when instructed to work in the ...ree loops of the same row, work in ...hese loops *(Fig. 2)*.

...ig. 2

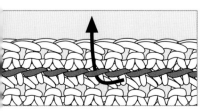

POST STITCH

Work around post of stitch indicated, inserting hook in direction of arrow *(Fig. 3)*.

Fig. 3

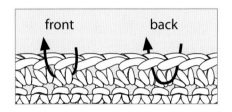

POPCORN (uses one st or sp)

Work 4 sts in st or sp indicated, drop loop from hook, insert hook in first st of 4-dc group, hook dropped loop and draw through *(Fig. 4)*, ch 1 to close.

Fig. 4

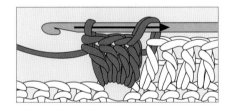

REVERSE SINGLE CROCHET

(abbreviated reverse sc)

Working from **left** to **right**, ★ insert hook in st to **right** of hook *(Fig. 5a)*, YO and draw through, under and to left of loop on hook (2 loops on hook) *(Fig. 5b)*, YO and draw through both loops on hook *(Fig. 5c)* (reverse sc made, *Fig. 5d*); repeat from ★ around.

Fig. 5a

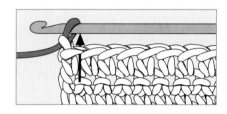

Fig. 5b

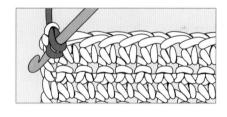

Fig. 5c

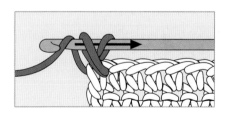

Fig. 5d

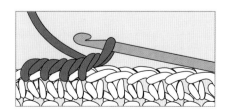

YARN INFORMATION

Each afghan in this leaflet was made using medium weight yarn. Any brand of medium weight yarn may be used. It is best to refer to the yardage/meters when determining how many balls or skeins to purchase. Remember, to achieve the same look, it is the weight of yarn that is important, not the brand of yarn. For your convenience, listed **below** are the specific yarns used to create our photography models.

BLACKBERRIES & CROSSES
Patons® Canadiana
#10343 Pale Amethyst

CHEVRONS & DIAMONDS
Caron® Simply Soft® Paints
#1 Tapestry

MOSS STITCH & CABLES
Plymouth Yarn® Jeannee Worsted
#15 Pale Pink

POPCORN DIAMONDS
Red Heart® Eco-Ways™
#1821 Blue Cloud

MEET BECKY STEVENS

Becky Stevens made the move from her home state of Pennsylvania to Maryland 43 years ago—which was about the time she started crocheting. She's learned so much about the skill since then that she teaches a weekly group in her home and holds an annual workshop at a New York lake resort.

Becky says, "I think the most rewarding things about crochet are relaxing with your project and seeing the final result, especially when making a very personal, thoughtful gift."

Your opinion matters!

WE WOULD LOVE TO HEAR if our online video instructions and the new format of our publications are helpful to you!

PLEASE SHARE your comments and suggestions at www.facebook.com/Official.LeisureArts

PRODUCTION TEAM: Technical Writers/Editors - Joan Beebe, Jean Guirguis, and Peggy Greig; Editorial Writer - Susan McManus Johnson; Senior Graphic Artist - Lora Puls; Graphic Artists - Becca Snider Tally and Dave Pope; Photo Stylist - Sondra Daniel; and Photographer - Ken West